omelets & frittatas

omelets & frittatas

Jennie Shapter   photography by Tara Fisher

RYLAND
PETERS
& SMALL

LONDON NEW YORK

First published in the
United States in 2005
by Ryland Peters & Small, Inc.
519 Broadway, 5th Floor
New York, NY 10012
www.rylandpeters.com

10 9 8 7 6 5 4 3

Printed in China

Shapter, Jennie.
  Omelets & frittatas / Jennie Shapter ;
photography by Tara Fisher.
     p. cm.
  Includes index.
  ISBN 10: 1-84172-818-7
  ISBN 13: 978-1-84172-818-6
  1. Omelets. I. Title.
TX745.S495 2005
641.6'75--dc22

2004021091

Senior Designer Steve Painter
Commissioning Editor
   Elsa Petersen-Schepelern
Editor Susah Stuck
Production Sheila Smith
Art Director Gabriella Le Grazie
Publishing Director Alison Starling

Food Stylist Jennie Shapter
Stylist Paul Hopper

Notes

• All spoon measurements are level
unless otherwise specified.
• All eggs are large or extra-large, as
specified. Uncooked or partially cooked
eggs should not be served to the very
young, the very old, those with
compromised immune systems, or
to pregnant women.

Author's note

Unfortunately eggs are susceptible to
salmonella and as a safeguard it is
recommended that we eat only eggs that
are well cooked and have no trace of
softness. Salmonella is not present in all
eggs and, while it must be taken very
seriously, I am still prepared to accept
the slight risk of a soft, creamy middle in
the center of my own omelets, but the
decision is yours.

   However, as a general rule, people at
risk, such as the elderly, the very young,
pregnant women, and anyone recovering
from a serious illness, should be aware
and avoid French-style omelets (see note
left). Tortillas and frittatas are fine, but
double check that they are completely
cooked in the center before serving.

contents

breakfast or brunch, lunch, or a light supper …

Is there anyone who doesn't enjoy a well-made omelet? The light and airy French-style omelet is one of the quickest of all meals. An Italian frittata or Spanish tortilla may take a little longer, but the process is much more relaxed, leaving you time to chat or sip a glass of wine. Frittatas and tortillas are also easier to make when serving several people. These flat omelets are extremely versatile, served hot or cold as snacks, for main meals, light lunch or supper dishes, for picnics, or even between slices of crusty bread.

Where possible, buy free-range or organic eggs with bright yellow yolks. Buy the very best quality and, above all, make sure the eggs are fresh. The flavor of the omelet will be affected by the quality of the eggs.

Many of the French omelet recipes have been written for one person or two to three for a snack or light meal, while the tortillas serve two, four or even more people. It is difficult to be exact, as it all depends on when you are serving them and how big an appetite you have. If you have any leftover tortilla or frittata, it can be eaten cold the next day, although I find the plate always seems to end up empty, no matter the number of servings.

omelet know-how

Choosing the right equipment

Omelets are easy to make, but it is essential to use the right equipment. One of the secrets of a good omelet is the pan. Regardless of the type of omelet you are making, the size, shape, and material from which the pan is made are extremely important and, ideally, you should keep that pan exclusively for omelet making.

A French omelet pan has a curved edge, making it easier to turn the omelet out onto the plate. For a tortilla or frittata, a large skillet with sloping sides is best.

Choose a heavy-based pan or skillet, either cast iron, aluminum, or nonstick—everyone has their favorite. If you choose cast iron or aluminum, it must be well seasoned first, otherwise the eggs will stick. A nonstick pan solves this problem, but you must use non-scratch tools to avoid damaging the surface. Whichever you choose, it must have a heavy base, because a thin base doesn't disperse the heat evenly. Avoid stainless steel; though attractive, it is not a good conductor of heat.

To season a pan or skillet, follow the instructions supplied with it. If there aren't any, fill it with about ½-inch depth of cooking oil and heat gently until hot, reduce to a low heat for about 30 minutes, then let cool. Repeat, then discard the oil and wipe off any excess with paper towels.

Some omelets, such as soufflés, oven-baked omelets, tortillas, and frittatas, are finished under the broiler or in the oven, so it is essential to use a pan with a heatproof or removable handle. Remember that the handle will be hot, so make sure you hold it with an oven mitt.

The size of the pan is equally important—too small and the omelet will be too thick and will not fold; too large and the eggs will be thin and leathery. I have given a guideline of pan and skillet sizes for small (7 inches), medium (8 inches) and large (10 inches) in the recipes, but these can be varied slightly by about ½ inch either way. It is important to measure the base of the pan, not the top, as is often quoted on the packaging of a new pan.

Making the omelet …

All cooks have their favorite omelet-cooking method. The first decision is the choice of cooking medium—oil or unsalted butter. Whichever you choose, make sure you heat it gently and swirl it around the base and the sides of the pan before adding the eggs, to keep them from sticking. For French omelets, I like to use butter or a combination of butter and safflower oil. Butter imparts a rich flavor, but will burn easily, so be careful—adding a little oil will help. For tortillas and frittatas, oil is more

common—either extra virgin olive oil or safflower oil. Again, your preference for flavor will probably dictate which you use. I prefer olive oil to impart a flavor in recipes such as the classic potato tortilla where the potatoes almost stew in the oil.

French omelets should be made quickly, drawing the egg mixture from the edges to the center, until the eggs are cooked but still creamy in the middle. Preferred utensils include the back or flat of a fork or a tablespoon, though a spatula can also be used.

Use the spatula to loosen the edges of a tortilla or frittata before turning or removing from the skillet. To finish cooking a tortilla, you should turn it over in the skillet so you will need a large, flat plate or saucepan lid. Shake the skillet to check that the tortilla is not stuck to the bottom before setting the plate or lid over the top. Hold the skillet with one hand and the plate or lid with the other. Turn both over together so the tortilla drops onto the plate. Use the spatula to help ease the tortilla back into the skillet.

Pan and skillet care

If your pan is a seasoned aluminum or cast iron pan or skillet, don't wash it after cooking an omelet. After each use, wipe it well with a damp cloth or a paper towel. If anything should stick to the pan, rub it off with a paper towel dipped in a little salt.

The mixture

The success of a good omelet is often in the correct mixing of the eggs. Break them up with a fork, rather than beating fiercely with a whisk, which would make the eggs too liquid, spoil their texture, and produce a heavy, leathery omelet. Under- rather than overbeating is the secret of success.

Herbs will taste even better if you pick them just before cooking, so if you grow your own, this is the perfect omelet for you. You can vary them to suit what you have available, just make sure that if you include powerful varieties like sage or mint, use less, while more subtle types such as chervil can be increased.

summer herb omelet

3 extra-large eggs

1 tablespoon snipped fresh chives

2 tablespoons chopped fresh dill

1 tablespoon chopped fresh tarragon

2 teaspoons unsalted butter

fresh herbs such as chives and chive flowers or a handful of basil, to serve

sea salt and freshly ground black pepper

a 7-inch heavy omelet pan (measure the base, not the top)

serves 1

Break the eggs into a bowl and season with a little salt and pepper. Beat lightly with a fork, just enough to mix the yolks and whites. Mix in the chives, dill, and tarragon.

Melt the butter in the omelet pan over medium-high heat and swirl it around to coat the bottom and sides of the pan. When the butter starts to foam, pour in the eggs.

Using a spatula or the back of a fork, draw the mixture from the sides to the center as it sets. Let the liquid flow and fill the space at the sides and, at the same time, tip the pan backwards and forwards.

After a short time, the omelet will be cooked but still creamy in the center. Tilt the pan and fold over a third of the omelet towards the center, then fold over again, slide onto a warmed plate and serve immediately with extra herbs.

Variations

Cheese omelet Omit the herbs and add 2 tablespoons grated Cheddar cheese. Sprinkle 1 tablespoon grated cheese over the omelet before folding.

Mushroom omelet Omit the herbs. Before making the omelet, cook about ½ cup chopped mushrooms gently in a little oil or butter for about 10 minutes, until all the excess moisture has evaporated. Sprinkle over the omelet before folding.

omelets

A strong blue cheese such as Roquefort adds a powerful flavor to this omelet, which I love. However, if you prefer a more delicate flavor, try using smooth, creamy-textured dolcelatte, or a mountain Gorgonzola. Both these cheeses are quite soft and will not crumble like Roquefort, so are best chopped into small pieces before adding.

caramelized onion and blue cheese omelet

1 tablespoon unsalted butter

1 tablespoon safflower oil

1 small onion, halved and thinly sliced

3 extra-large eggs

½ cup (2 oz.) crumbled blue cheese such as Roquefort

sea salt and freshly ground black pepper

a 7-inch heavy omelet pan (measure the base, not the top)

serves 1

Put half the butter and oil in the omelet pan and heat until the butter has melted. Add the onion and sauté gently for about 10 minutes, until golden and caramelized, stirring occasionally.

Meanwhile, break the eggs into a bowl and beat lightly with a fork, just enough to mix the yolks and whites. Season with salt and pepper. Using a slotted spoon, add the onions to the eggs and mix gently.

Increase the heat to medium-high and add the remaining butter and oil if necessary. When the pan is hot, pour in the omelet mixture. Using a spatula or the back of a fork, draw the mixture from the sides to the center as it sets. Let the liquid flow and fill the space at the sides and, at the same time, tip the pan backwards and forwards.

Sprinkle the cheese over the top, fold over a third of the omelet to the center, then fold over the remaining third. Slide onto a warmed plate and serve immediately.

It is important to start folding the omelet while it is still slightly liquid in the center to avoid it overcooking and becoming tough and leathery. Make sure the person who is going to eat it is ready first, rather than the omelet.

smoked salmon omelet

3 oz. smoked salmon, cut into thin strips

1 tablespoon milk

3 extra-large eggs

2 teaspoons unsalted butter

2 tablespoons sour cream or crème fraîche

1 tablespoon chopped fresh dill

sea salt and freshly ground black pepper

a 7-inch heavy omelet pan (measure the base, not the top)

serves 1

Put half the smoked salmon in a bowl, add the milk, and let stand for 15 minutes.

Break the eggs into a bowl and beat lightly with a fork, just enough to mix the yolks and whites. Season with salt and plenty of pepper, then stir in the milk and smoked salmon.

Heat the butter in the omelet pan. When the butter starts to foam, pour in the egg mixture and cook over medium-high heat, drawing the mixture from the sides to the center as it sets. Let the liquid flow and fill the space at the sides.

After a short time, the omelet will be cooked but still creamy in the center. Top the omelet with the sour cream and sprinkle with chopped dill and the remaining smoked salmon.

Fold over one-third of the omelet to the center, then fold over the remaining third, slide onto a warmed plate, and serve immediately.

Variation This omelet can also be made with 2 extra-large eggs, using a 6-inch omelet pan (measured at the base, not the top).

There is nothing quite like the flavor of fresh crab, but if it isn't available, use frozen crabmeat. Make sure you drain it well before adding to the omelet. This recipe would work equally well with shrimp.

asian crab omelet

3 extra-large eggs

1 teaspoon Thai fish sauce or soy sauce

freshly ground black pepper

1 tablespoon chopped cilantro

½ cup (2 oz.) lump crabmeat, fresh or frozen and thawed

5 teaspoons safflower oil

1 small chile, seeded and chopped

3 scallions, finely sliced

a 7-inch heavy omelet pan (measure the base, not the top)

serves 1

Break the eggs into a bowl and beat lightly with a fork, just enough to mix the yolks and whites. Stir in the fish sauce and season with pepper. Mix the cilantro and crabmeat in a bowl and set aside.

Heat 1 tablespoon of the oil in the omelet pan, add the chile and three-fourths of the scallions, then stir-fry for 1 minute. Remove from the pan with a slotted spoon and stir into the eggs.

Add the remaining oil to the pan, heat for a few seconds, then pour in the egg mixture. Tip the pan to spread the eggs evenly over the base, leave for 5 seconds, then draw the edges of the omelet to the center, letting the liquid egg flow to the sides and at the same time tipping the pan backwards and forwards.

After a short time, the omelet will be cooked but still creamy in the center. Sprinkle the cilantro and crabmeat mixture over the omelet. Tilt the pan, fold one-third of the omelet towards the center, then fold over again and transfer to a warmed plate. Serve immediately sprinkled with the remaining scallions.

Ideal for a lunch or supper dish, or perfect for al fresco dining served with a crisp salad, this omelet is just bursting with flavor. It is worth buying tomatoes ripened on the vine for their extra taste explosion.

feta cheese and tomato open omelet

5 extra-large eggs

2 tablespoons chopped fresh basil

1 tablespoon chopped fresh mint

3 scallions, finely chopped

2 tablespoons safflower oil

¾ cup (3 oz.) crumbled feta cheese

8 small cherry tomatoes, halved

sea salt and freshly ground black pepper

a 7-inch heavy omelet pan (measure the base, not the top)

serves 2

Break the eggs into a bowl and beat lightly with a fork, just enough to mix the yolks and whites. Season with salt and pepper, add 2 tablespoons water, the basil, mint, and scallions and mix briefly.

Heat the oil in the omelet pan. Pour in the egg mixture and cook over medium heat for 4–5 minutes, drawing the mixture from the sides to the center until the omelet is half cooked.

Top with the feta and the tomato halves, cut side up, and cook for 2 minutes. Slide under a preheated broiler and cook until light golden brown. Slide onto a warmed plate and serve immediately.

A fusion of tortilla-inspired wraps with Portuguese-style piri-piri chicken. Piri-piri is a hot sauce made from serrano chiles; increase or reduce the amount of sauce in the marinade depending on how hot you would like it.

omelet wraps

2 tablespoons extra virgin olive oil

freshly squeezed juice of 1 lime

2 tablespoons chopped cilantro

1 tablespoon piri-piri sauce, or 2–3 dashes Tabasco

2 skinless chicken breasts, cut into thin strips

5 large eggs

2 tablespoons milk

2 tablespoons finely snipped fresh chives

1 avocado, halved, pitted, peeled, and chopped

6 cherry tomatoes, quartered

4 teaspoons unsalted butter

sea salt and freshly ground black pepper

a nonstick skillet

a 7-inch heavy omelet pan (measure the base, not the top)

serves 2

Put the olive oil, lime juice, and cilantro in a bowl and mix with a fork. Put half the mixture in a shallow dish, add the piri-piri sauce, and mix well. Add the chicken and stir to coat with the marinade. Set aside for 30 minutes.

Break the eggs into a bowl, then add the milk, salt, and pepper. Beat lightly with a fork, just enough to mix the yolks and whites. Mix in the chives. Add the avocado, cherry tomatoes, the remaining olive oil, and lime juice and stir gently to coat.

Stir-fry the chicken in a nonstick skillet for 3–4 minutes, or until the juices run clear, then remove from the heat and set aside.

Meanwhile melt half the butter in the omelet pan over medium-high heat and swirl it around to coat the bottom and sides of the pan. When the butter starts to foam, pour in half the eggs.

Tip the pan to spread the eggs evenly over the base, leave for 5 seconds, then draw the edges of the eggs to the center, letting the liquid egg flow to the sides. When the omelet has just set, transfer to a warm plate, add the remaining butter to the pan, and cook the second omelet in the same way.

Mix the cooked chicken with the avocado and tomatoes and divide between the two omelets, spooning the mixture in a line down the middle. Roll up the omelets, cut in half, and serve.

Note An excellent source for piri-piri and other quality Portuguese ingredients is www.saldemar. com.

A soufflé omelet is quite simple to prepare and results in an amazingly light and fluffy dish that just melts in the mouth. This one is finished with Taleggio cheese, which oozes out of the center as you cut into it.

cheese and watercress soufflé omelet

4 extra-large eggs, separated

½ cup (2 oz.) grated sharp Cheddar cheese

½ cup chopped watercress

2 oz. Taleggio cheese

2 tablespoons unsalted butter

1 small red onion, finely chopped

2 tablespoons freshly grated Parmesan cheese

sea salt and freshly ground black pepper

a 7-inch heavy skillet (measure the base, not the top)

serves 2

Put the egg yolks in a large bowl, add the grated Cheddar, watercress, salt, and pepper and mix well. Cut the Taleggio into thin slices, then in half crosswise.

Put the skillet over medium heat. Add half the butter, heat until melted, add the onion, and cook for 4–5 minutes, or until softened. Remove with a slotted spoon and stir into the egg yolk mixture. Preheat the broiler to the highest setting.

Put the egg whites in a very clean bowl and whisk until soft peaks form. Fold into the egg yolk mixture. Add the remaining butter to the skillet, increase the heat to medium-high, and as soon as the butter is foaming, pile the omelet mixture into the skillet and gently shake it to even out the mixture. Cook for 2 minutes, or until pale gold on the underside.

Top with the Taleggio and slide under a preheated broiler to melt the cheese and finish cooking the top of the omelet. Fold in half, transfer to a warmed plate, and serve immediately, sprinkled with the Parmesan.

4 extra-large eggs

2 tablespoons plain yogurt

1 teaspoon ground cumin

2 tablespoons chopped cilantro

1 garlic clove, crushed

2 tablespoons safflower oil

1 onion, finely chopped

1 small red chile,
seeded and chopped

1-inch piece of fresh ginger,
peeled and grated

2 tomatoes, finely chopped

sea salt and freshly
ground black pepper

cucumber raita

about 3 inches cucumber, peeled

⅔ cup plain yogurt

2 scallions, finely chopped

1 tablespoon chopped cilantro

1 teaspoon freshly squeezed
lime juice

sea salt and freshly
ground black pepper

*a 7-inch heavy omelet pan
(measure the base, not the top)*

serves 2–3

Eggs, while not particularly common in Indian cooking, are adored by the Parsee community of Bombay, especially when made into a spicy, aromatic omelet. It is served like a Spanish omelet, hot or cold, cut into wedges, often with chutney or a raita (yogurt salad) on the side. I like this cool cucumber raita because it complements the spicy flavors of the ginger and chile.

indian omelet

To make the cucumber raita, coarsely grate the cucumber and squeeze out the excess moisture. Put in a bowl, then stir in the yogurt, scallions, cilantro, lime juice, salt, and pepper. Chill.

To make the omelet, break the eggs into a bowl, add the yogurt, and beat lightly with a fork. Stir in the cumin, cilantro, garlic, salt, and pepper.

Heat 1 tablespoon of the oil in the omelet pan. Add the onion, chile, and ginger and sauté over medium-high heat for 2–3 minutes, then add the tomatoes and cook for 1–2 minutes. Using a slotted spoon, transfer to the egg mixture and stir gently.

Add the remaining oil to the pan and swirl it around to coat the bottom and sides. Pour the egg mixture into the pan, reduce the heat to low, and cook for about 5–6 minutes, or until the underside is golden and the top has almost set.

Slide under a preheated broiler to finish cooking or put a plate or flat saucepan lid on top of the skillet, then invert so the omelet drops onto the plate or lid. Slide back into the pan and cook for 1–2 minutes. Cut into wedges and serve with a spoonful of raita.

This is a great way to cook an omelet—once prepared, it can finish cooking in the oven, making the whole thing quite relaxed. It is ideal for a late, lazy breakfast, but good enough to eat at any time of the day. Make sure the skillet handle is ovenproof or removable.

baked brunch omelet

2 tablespoons safflower oil

4 slices smoked bacon, cut into strips

1 onion, finely sliced

1 medium potato, peeled and cubed

1½ cups (3 oz.) sliced small white mushrooms

5 extra-large eggs

scant ½ cup milk

¾ cup (3 oz.) grated sharp Cheddar cheese

1 tablespoon unsalted butter

1 tablespoon freshly grated Parmesan cheese

sea salt and freshly ground black pepper

an 8-inch heavy nonstick skillet (measure the base, not the top)

serves 2–3

Preheat the oven to 400°F. Heat the oil in the skillet, add the bacon, onion, and potato, and sauté for 6 minutes, or until the potatoes start to brown. Add the mushrooms and sauté for 2 minutes.

Meanwhile, break the eggs into a large bowl, add the milk, and beat lightly with a fork, just enough to mix the yolks and whites. Season with salt and plenty of pepper. Stir in three-fourths of the Cheddar.

Using a slotted spoon, transfer the potato mixture to the bowl of eggs and mix well. Add the butter to the skillet and, when it starts to foam, pour in the omelet mixture. Sprinkle with the remaining cheese and transfer to the preheated oven.

Cook for 12–15 minutes, or until just set. Loosen the edges with a spatula and slide onto a warmed serving plate. Sprinkle with Parmesan and serve immediately.

This is a great way to use up leftover spaghetti. I have mixed it with a fresh arrabbiata sauce made with tomatoes and chiles to add a fiery flavor.

spaghetti and arugula frittata

3 tablespoons extra virgin olive oil

1 onion, chopped

1 garlic clove, crushed

3 ripe plum tomatoes, chopped

1 fresh red chile, seeded and finely chopped

2 tablespoons tomato paste

⅔ cup white wine or water

2–2½ cups cold cooked spaghetti (5 oz. before cooking)

6 extra-large eggs

2 tablespoons freshly grated Parmesan cheese

a small handful of arugula

2 tablespoons balsamic vinegar

sea salt and freshly ground black pepper

a 12-inch heavy nonstick skillet (measure the base, not the top)

serves 4

Heat 1 tablespoon of the oil in a saucepan, add the onion, and sauté for 5 minutes until softened. Add the garlic, tomatoes, and chile and cook for 3–4 minutes, stirring several times. Add the tomato paste and wine or water and simmer for 5 minutes. Remove from the heat, add the spaghetti, and toss gently.

Break the eggs into a large bowl and beat lightly with a fork. Add the spaghetti and sauce and mix gently.

Heat the remaining oil in the skillet, add the spaghetti and egg mixture, and cook over low heat for 10–12 minutes, or until golden brown on the underside and almost set on the top.

Sprinkle with the Parmesan and slide under a preheated broiler for 30–60 seconds to melt the cheese and finish cooking the top. Let cool for 5 minutes, then transfer to a plate. Put the arugula on top of the frittata, sprinkle with balsamic vinegar, and serve.

italian frittatas

Porcini are difficult to buy fresh, but are widely available dried. They are one of the best mushrooms, with an intense, rich flavor that will pervade the omelet. Strain the soaking liquid from the porcini and add a spoonful to the omelet mixture, or keep it for a soup or stew.

porcini frittata

½ oz. dried porcini mushrooms

6 large eggs

3 tablespoons mascarpone cheese

3 tablespoons chopped fresh flat-leaf parsley

3 tablespoons extra virgin olive or safflower oil

1 onion, halved and sliced

2½ cups (4 oz.) sliced small white mushrooms

1 tablespoon freshly grated Parmesan cheese

1 tablespoon unsalted butter

3 oz. fresh wild mushrooms

sea salt and freshly ground black pepper

an 8-inch heavy nonstick skillet (measure the base, not the top)

serves 2–3

Put the porcini in a small bowl and cover with warm water. Let soak for 30 minutes. Break 1 of the eggs into a bowl, add the mascarpone, and mix well. Add the remaining eggs and beat lightly with a fork. Stir in the parsley and season with salt and pepper.

Heat 1 tablespoon of the oil in the skillet, add the onion, and cook over low heat until soft. Add another tablespoon of oil and the mushrooms and cook for 5 minutes. Drain the porcini and chop if large. Add to the skillet and cook for 2 minutes.

Using a slotted spoon, transfer the mushrooms and onions to the eggs and mix gently.

Wipe out the skillet with a paper towel, add the remaining oil, and heat gently. Add the frittata mixture and cook over low heat until browned on the underside and nearly set on top. Sprinkle with Parmesan and slide under a preheated broiler to finish cooking the top and melt the cheese. Transfer to a warm serving plate.

Melt the butter in the skillet, add the wild mushrooms, and sauté quickly. Spoon over the top of the frittata and serve.

Baby spinach is essential for this recipe because the leaves wilt and soften quickly, so you needn't remove the stalks or chop the leaves. Italian bacon (pancetta) adds a special depth of flavor. Like all frittatas, this one is wonderful to take on a picnic or as a bag lunch.

spinach and pancetta frittata

6 extra-large eggs

1 tablespoon extra virgin olive or safflower oil

4 oz. smoked Italian bacon (pancetta), cut into cubes, or bacon cut into strips

4 scallions, chopped

1 garlic clove, finely chopped

1½ cups (6 oz.) baby spinach

sea salt and freshly ground black pepper

a 12-inch heavy skillet (measure the base, not the top)

serves 4

Break the eggs into a bowl and beat lightly with a fork. Season well with salt and plenty of pepper.

Heat 1 tablespoon of the oil in the skillet. Add the bacon and cook over medium heat for 3–4 minutes until it starts to brown.

Add the scallions, garlic, and spinach and stir-fry for 3–4 minutes or until the spinach has wilted and the onions have softened.

Pour the egg mixture into the pan, quickly mix into the other ingredients, and stop stirring. Reduce to a low heat and cook for 8–10 minutes, or until the top has almost set. Slide under a preheated broiler to finish cooking the top, then serve hot or cold, cut into wedges.

This frittata has a real Mediterranean feel and is flavored with some of Italy's favorite ingredients—olives, sun-dried tomatoes, and Parmesan. If you have the time, it is worth mixing the tomatoes and sage into the eggs up to an hour before cooking for a more intense flavor.

sun-dried tomato and parmesan frittata

6 extra-large eggs

8 sun-dried tomatoes in oil, drained and sliced

1 tablespoon chopped fresh sage leaves

⅓ cup thickly sliced pitted black olives

½ cup (2 oz.) freshly grated Parmesan cheese, plus extra shavings to serve (optional)

2 tablespoons extra virgin olive oil

1 onion, halved and sliced

sea salt and freshly ground black pepper

an 8-inch nonstick skillet (measure the base, not the top)

serves 2–3

Break the eggs into a large bowl and beat lightly with a fork. Add the sun-dried tomatoes, sage, olives, Parmesan, salt, and pepper and mix gently.

Heat the oil in the skillet, add the onion, and cook over low heat until soft and golden.

Increase the heat to moderate, pour the egg mixture into the skillet, and stir just long enough to mix in the onion. Cook over medium-low heat until the base of the frittata is golden and the top has almost set.

Slide the skillet under a preheated broiler to finish cooking, or put a plate or flat saucepan lid on top of the skillet, then invert so the frittata drops onto the plate or lid. Return the frittata to the skillet, cooked side up, and cook on top of the stove for 1–2 minutes.

Transfer to a serving plate, top with Parmesan shavings, if using, and serve hot or cold, cut into wedges.

The frittata is Italy's version of a flat, open-faced omelet and this one is simply flavored with fresh mint and zucchini. The zucchini can be coarsely grated rather than sliced, but make sure you squeeze out any excess water first before adding to the skillet.

minted zucchini frittata

6 extra-large eggs

2 tablespoons chopped fresh mint

8 oz. baby new potatoes, thickly sliced

2 tablespoons extra virgin olive or safflower oil

1 large onion, chopped

4 zucchini, sliced

sea salt and freshly ground black pepper

a 12-inch heavy skillet (measure the base, not the top)

serves 3–4

Break the eggs into a bowl and beat them lightly with a fork. Season well with salt and pepper. Mix in the chopped mint.

Cook the potatoes in a saucepan of boiling, salted water until just tender. Drain thoroughly.

Meanwhile, heat the oil in the skillet, add the onion, and cook gently for about 10 minutes, until soft and pale golden. Add the zucchini and stir over low heat for 3–4 minutes until just softened. Add the potatoes and mix gently.

Pour the eggs over the vegetables and cook over low heat until the frittata is lightly browned underneath and almost set on top. Slide under a preheated broiler for 30–60 seconds to set the top. Serve, cut into wedges.

Pecorino is the generic name for all Italian cheeses made from sheeps' milk. Pecorino Romano from Lazio, the region around Rome, is one of the best known and probably Italy's oldest cheese. It has a sharp, dry flavor and a hard texture, perfect for grating, which makes it the best choice for this recipe.

asparagus, pecorino, and prosciutto frittata

6 asparagus spears, about 4 oz., cut into short lengths

3 cups (8 oz.) frozen fava beans or 2 cups frozen peas, thawed

6 extra-large eggs

¾ cup (3 oz.) freshly grated pecorino cheese

3 tablespoons chopped fresh oregano

1 tablespoon chopped fresh flat-leaf parsley

2 tablespoons extra virgin olive or safflower oil

1 medium onion, chopped

3 thin slices prosciutto

sea salt and freshly ground black pepper

a 12-inch heavy nonstick skillet (measure the base, not the top)

serves 3–4

Put the asparagus in a saucepan of boiling water and cook for about 5–6 minutes, or until just tender. Refresh in cold running water and drain thoroughly. If using fava beans, remove the waxy skins and discard.

Break the eggs into a large bowl and beat lightly with a fork. Season with salt and pepper and mix in two-thirds of the cheese, all the oregano, parsley, asparagus, and fava beans or peas.

Heat the oil in the skillet, add the onion, and cook over medium heat for 5 minutes, or until just starting to brown. Pour the frittata mixture into the skillet and briefly stir in the onion. Reduce the heat to low and cook for 12–15 minutes, or until the frittata is golden brown underneath and almost set on top.

Sprinkle with the remaining pecorino. Tear the slices of proscuitto into 2–3 pieces and arrange on top of the frittata. Slide under a preheated broiler for 2–3 minutes to melt the cheese and frizzle the prosciutto. Loosen the edges with a spatula and slide onto a warm plate.

A frittata should be cooked slowly, only lightly colored, and still slightly moist when served. The Italians usually flip it to finish cooking, but often a recipe will suggest quickly flashing the frittata under the broiler or putting it in a hot oven just to set the top. I prefer the broiler, but use whichever method you find easiest.

grilled bell pepper frittata

1 small red bell pepper, quartered and seeded

1 small yellow bell pepper, quartered and seeded

1 small green bell pepper, quartered and seeded

2 tablespoons ricotta or mascarpone cheese

6 extra-large eggs

2 tablespoons fresh thyme leaves

2 tablespoons extra virgin olive or safflower oil

1 large red onion, sliced

1 tablespoon balsamic vinegar

2 garlic cloves, crushed

sea salt and freshly ground black pepper

an 8-inch heavy skillet (measure the base, not the top)

serves 2–3

Put the bell peppers skin side up under a preheated broiler and cook until the skins have blackened. Transfer to a bowl, cover, and let cool. This will steam off the skins, making them easier to remove.

Put the cheese in a large bowl, add 1 egg, and mix to loosen the cheese. Beat in the remaining eggs with a fork. Season with salt, pepper, and thyme and stir into the cheese mixture.

Peel the blackened skins off the bell peppers and rinse under cold running water. Pat dry with paper towels and cut into thick strips. Stir into the bowl.

Heat half the oil in the skillet, add the sliced onion and balsamic vinegar, and cook over gentle heat for about 10 minutes until softened. Add the garlic and cook for 1 minute.

Using a slotted spoon, add the onion to the egg mixture, and stir. Add the remaining oil to the pan and heat gently. Pour the frittata mixture into the pan and let cook over low heat until almost set, puffy, and light golden-brown on the underside.

Finish under a preheated broiler or put a plate or flat saucepan lid on top of the skillet, then invert so the frittata drops onto the plate or lid. Slide back into the skillet, cooked side up, and cook for 30–60 seconds. Transfer to a serving plate and serve hot or at room temperature, cut into wedges.

1 cup (8 oz.) broccoli florets

6 extra-large eggs

3 tablespoons extra virgin olive oil

1 large onion, chopped

1 garlic clove, crushed

1 red chile, seeded
and finely chopped

4 oz. cooked peeled shrimp,
cut into pieces if large

3 oz. mozzarella cheese, cubed

sea salt and freshly
ground black pepper

Parmesan shavings, to serve
(optional)

pesto sauce

1½ cups basil leaves

1 garlic clove, chopped

2 tablespoons pine nuts

⅓ cup freshly grated
Parmesan cheese

½ cup extra virgin olive oil

sea salt and freshly
ground black pepper

*a 12-inch heavy nonstick skillet
(measure the base, not the top)*

serves 3–4

Basil, with its intense spicy scent and pungent sweet flavor, is a cornerstone of Mediterranean cooking, and is the main ingredient for pesto sauce. You can use ready-made pesto, but it really is worth that little extra effort to make it yourself and capture the redolence of the fresh herb.

mozzarella and shrimp frittata with pesto

To make the pesto sauce, put the basil in a blender or food processor, add the garlic, pine nuts, grated Parmesan, olive oil, salt, and pepper and blend until creamy. Set aside.

Put the broccoli in a saucepan of boiling, salted water and cook until barely tender. Drain and refresh under cold running water, then drain again thoroughly.

Break the eggs into a bowl, add salt and pepper, beat lightly with a fork, and set aside. Heat the oil in the skillet, add the onion, and cook for 5 minutes, stirring frequently. Add the garlic and chile and sauté for 2 minutes, stirring frequently. Stir in the broccoli and shrimp.

Pour the egg mixture into the pan, making sure it reaches the edges. Dot the cubes of mozzarella over the top. Cook over low heat until almost set, then slide under a preheated broiler for 1–2 minutes, until the top has set and the cheese is bubbling. Let cool slightly, then serve cut into wedges. Trickle pesto sauce over the top, add the Parmesan shavings, if using, and serve.

This classic tortilla consists of just three ingredients: eggs, potatoes, and onions. Together, they are transformed into an unbelievably delicious dish. Tortillas may be cut into squares or wedges and eaten for lunch or supper, as a snack or for a picnic, or even between chunks of bread— a favorite way in Spain. You can also cut it into smaller squares and serve it as tapas with cocktails.

classic spanish tortilla

1 large onion

3–4 tablespoons extra virgin olive or safflower oil

4 medium peeled potatoes, about 1 lb.

5 extra-large eggs

sea salt and freshly ground black pepper

an 8-inch heavy nonstick skillet (measure the base, not the top)

serves 2–3

Cut the onion in half, then slice thinly lengthwise and separate into slivers. Heat 3 tablespoons of the oil in the skillet.

Thinly slice the potatoes, then add them to the skillet in layers, alternating with the onion. Cook for 10–15 minutes over medium-low heat, lifting and turning occasionally, until just tender. The potatoes and onions should not brown very much.

Meanwhile, break the eggs into a large bowl, beat lightly with a fork, and season with salt and pepper. Remove the potatoes and onions from the skillet and drain in a colander, reserving any oil. Add the vegetables to the bowl of eggs and mix gently.

Heat the reserved oil in the skillet, adding a little extra if necessary. Add the potato and egg mixture, spreading it evenly. Cook over medium-low heat until the bottom is golden brown and the top almost set.

Put a plate or flat saucepan lid on top of the skillet, then invert so the tortilla drops onto the plate or lid. Slide back into the skillet, brown side up, and cook on top of the stove for 2–3 minutes until the other side is lightly browned. Turn again and transfer to a serving plate, with the most attractive side upward. Serve hot or at room temperature, cut into wedges.

Note For authentic Spanish ingredients try www.tienda.com.

spanish tortillas

A robust omelet packed full of goodness makes a perfect recipe for using up small quantities of leftover ingredients, including vegetables such as broccoli, corn, lima beans, or mushrooms. I like to finish this tortilla under the broiler to retain the lovely colors on the top when serving, but you can also turn it over in the skillet to finish cooking in the classic way.

hearty country-style tortilla

¼ cup extra virgin olive or safflower oil

3 medium potatoes, about 12 oz., cubed

1 onion, halved and sliced

about ½ cup (3 oz.) green beans, trimmed and cut into three

4 asparagus spears, cut into 2-inch lengths

1 red bell pepper, quartered, seeded, and thinly sliced

3 oz. spicy chorizo, sliced

1 garlic clove, finely chopped

6 extra-large eggs

½ cup frozen peas

sea salt and freshly ground black pepper

a 12-inch heavy nonstick skillet (measure the base, not the top)

serves 4–6

Heat 2 tablespoons of the oil in the skillet. Add the potatoes and cook over medium heat for 5 minutes. Add the onion and cook for 10 minutes or until the potatoes are almost tender, lifting and turning occasionally.

Meanwhile put the beans and asparagus in a saucepan of boiling, salted water and cook for 5 minutes. Drain and refresh in cold water. Drain well.

Add the bell pepper, chorizo, asparagus, beans, and garlic to the potatoes and cook for 5 minutes, stirring frequently.

Break the eggs into a large bowl, add salt and pepper, and beat lightly with a fork. Mix in the peas and cooked vegetable mixture.

If necessary, wipe out the skillet with a paper towel, then add the remaining oil and heat until hot. Add the tortilla mixture, letting it spread evenly in the pan.

Cook over medium-low heat for about 10 minutes until the bottom is golden brown and the top almost set. Slide under a preheated broiler to set and lightly brown the top. Transfer to a serving plate and serve hot or warm, cut into wedges.

Any tortilla can be served as tapas; however this recipe makes it even easier because it is cooked in the oven. If you want to make the tapas in advance, serve them cold or reheat for a few minutes in a medium oven. They are delicious served with a chilled fino or amontillado sherry.

mushroom and sweet bell pepper tortilla tapas

3 tablespoons extra virgin olive or safflower oil

2 medium potatoes, about 8 oz., thinly sliced

1 small onion, halved and thinly sliced

1½ cups (3 oz.) sliced small white mushrooms

1 orange bell pepper, halved, seeded, and cut into strips

5 extra-large eggs

2 teaspoons chopped fresh oregano

sea salt and freshly ground black pepper

an 8-inch shallow nonstick cake pan

a large heavy skillet

serves 4

Pour 1 tablespoon of the oil into the cake pan and put in a preheated oven at 400°F to heat.

Meanwhile, heat the remaining oil in a large skillet, add the sliced potatoes and onion, and cook over medium heat for about 15 minutes, turning occasionally, until almost tender. Add the mushrooms and bell pepper and cook for 5 minutes.

Break the eggs into a large bowl and beat lightly with a fork. Add the oregano and season with salt and pepper. Remove the vegetables from the skillet with a slotted spoon, add to the bowl of eggs, and stir gently.

Transfer to the preheated cake pan, return to the oven, and cook for 15–20 minutes, or until the egg is just set in the center. Let stand for 10 minutes, then serve warm, cut into small squares.

A speciality of the Alicante region of Valencia is an unusual meat paella finished with an omelet topping. For this mouthwatering tortilla, I have replaced the meat with the shellfish typical of Paella Valenciana.

paella tortilla

3 tablespoons extra virgin olive or safflower oil

6 oz. skinless chicken breast, cut into strips

1 medium onion, chopped

1 garlic clove, chopped

1 red bell pepper, halved, seeded, and sliced

2 tomatoes, chopped

½ cup short-grain Spanish rice, such as calasparra, or Italian risotto rice

a pinch of saffron threads, soaked in 2 tablespoons hot water

1 cup chicken stock

1½ cups (6 oz.) mixed seafood, such as shrimp, mussels, and squid rings

6 large eggs

3 tablespoons frozen peas, thawed

sea salt and freshly ground black pepper

a 12-inch heavy nonstick skillet (measure the base, not the top)

serves 4–6

Heat 2 tablespoons of the oil in the skillet, add the chicken, and sauté until browned. Transfer to a plate. Add the onion, garlic, and pepper and sauté for 5–6 minutes, stirring frequently, until softened.

Stir in the tomatoes, rice, and saffron and pour in the stock. Add the chicken and season with salt and plenty of black pepper. Cover and cook over gentle heat for about 20 minutes, or until the rice is almost tender, adding a little more stock if necessary.

Stir in the mixed seafood and cook for 5 minutes, or until the rice is just tender and all the liquid has been absorbed.

Break the eggs into a large bowl, add salt and pepper, and beat lightly with a fork. Stir in the paella mixture and the peas.

Wipe out the skillet with a paper towel. Heat the remaining oil in the skillet over medium heat, add the tortilla mixture, and cook over medium-low heat for 10–15 minutes, or until almost set.

Slide under a preheated broiler to set the top. Let stand for 5 minutes, then transfer to a serving plate and serve, cut into wedges.

Note If ready-mixed seafood cocktail is unavailable, use ½ cup each of shelled shrimp, shelled mussels, and squid rings.

Although potato is the traditional ingredient in a Spanish omelet, chickpeas are a delicious alternative, adding a slightly sweet, nutty flavor. This tortilla is quite filling, so is best as a main meal; I like to serve it with a crisp green salad and a glass of red wine.

chickpea tortilla

5 extra-large eggs

½ teaspoon sweet oak-smoked Spanish paprika

3 tablespoons chopped fresh flat-leaf parsley

3 tablespoons extra virgin olive oil

1 large onion, finely chopped

I red bell pepper, halved, seeded, and chopped

2 garlic cloves, finely chopped

2 cups (15 oz.) canned chickpeas (garbanzos), rinsed and well drained

sea salt and freshly ground black pepper

an 8-inch heavy nonstick skillet (measure the base, not the top)

serves 2–3

Break the eggs into a large bowl, add salt, pepper, and paprika, and beat lightly with a fork. Stir in the chopped parsley.

Heat 2 tablespoons of the oil in the skillet. Add the onion and bell pepper and cook for about 5 minutes until softened, turning frequently. Add the garlic and chickpeas and cook for 2 minutes.

Transfer to the bowl of eggs and stir gently. Add the remaining oil to the skillet and return to the heat. Add the chickpea mixture, spreading it evenly. Cook over medium-low heat until the bottom is golden brown and the top almost set.

Put a plate or flat saucepan lid on top of the skillet, then invert so the tortilla drops onto the plate or lid. Slide back into the skillet, brown side up, and cook for 2–3 minutes until lightly browned on the other side. Serve hot or at room temperature, cut into wedges.

Note For authentic Spanish ingredients, try www.tienda.com.

Most tortillas are inverted onto a plate and returned to the pan to finish cooking. However, this tortilla is topped with cured mountain ham and should be finished under the broiler. You can trickle a little extra virgin olive oil over the top before broiling and, for a truly extravagant touch, add a few slices of goat cheese log, which melts beautifully into the top of the tortilla.

tortilla with artichokes and serrano ham

3 tablespoons extra virgin olive or safflower oil

3 medium potatoes, about 12 oz., cubed

1 Spanish onion, chopped

5 extra-large eggs

2 cups (15 oz.) canned artichoke hearts or bottoms in water, well drained and cut in half

2 tablespoons fresh thyme leaves

3–4 oz. thinly sliced serrano ham or prosciutto, torn into strips

6–8 slices goat cheese log with rind, about 4 oz. (optional)

sea salt and freshly ground black pepper

a 12-inch heavy nonstick skillet (measure the base, not the top)

serves 3–4

Heat 2 tablespoons of the oil in the skillet. Add the potatoes and sauté over medium heat for about 5 minutes. Add the onion and cook for a further 10 minutes, lifting and turning occasionally, until just tender. The potatoes and onions should not brown very much.

Meanwhile, break the eggs into a large bowl, season with salt and pepper, and beat lightly with a fork.

Add the artichokes, thyme, and about three-fourths of the ham to the bowl. Add the potatoes and onion and stir gently.

Heat the remaining oil in the skillet. Add the tortilla mixture, spreading it evenly. Cook over medium-low heat for about 6 minutes, then top with the remaining ham. Cook for a further 4–5 minutes or until the bottom is golden brown and the top almost set.

Add the goat cheese, if using, and slide under a preheated broiler to brown the top, about 2–3 minutes. Serve the tortilla hot or warm, cut into wedges.

Buy deep orange sweet potatoes to achieve the best effect for this colorful tortilla. To melt the Brie, the tortilla is finished in the oven, so use a pan with a heatproof handle.

sweet potato and brie tortilla

2 medium sweet potatoes, about 1 lb., cut into chunks

¼ cup extra virgin olive or safflower oil

1 onion, halved lengthwise and sliced about ¼ inch thick

5 extra-large eggs

1 garlic clove, crushed

4 oz. Brie cheese

sea salt and freshly ground black pepper

a shallow roasting tray

an 8-inch heavy ovenproof skillet (measure the base, not the top)

serves 2–3

Put the potatoes and 2 tablespoons of the oil in the roasting tray and toss to coat. Roast in a preheated oven at 400°F for 15 minutes, then add the onion and mix well. Roast for a further 20 minutes, or until all the vegetables are tender.

Break the eggs into a large bowl and beat lightly with a fork. Stir in the salt, pepper, and garlic. Add the potatoes and onions and mix gently.

Heat the remaining oil in the skillet. Pour the tortilla mixture into the skillet and cook over medium-low heat for 6–8 minutes, or until set around the edges and is lightly browned underneath.

Slice the Brie and arrange on top of the tortilla. Return to the oven for 5 minutes, or until the Brie has melted and the top of the tortilla has set. Serve hot or warm, cut into wedges.

There are many variations of Eggah served throughout the Middle East, but Persian (Iranian) cuisine provides one of the finest. The flavor from copious quantities of fresh herbs bursts out as you bite into it. I like to add nuts for their interesting texture—if you have time, lightly toast the pine nuts first for a more intense flavor.

persian herb eggah

3 tablespoons safflower oil

1 medium onion, chopped

1 small eggplant, halved and sliced

1 garlic clove, crushed

5 extra-large eggs

⅓ cup chopped fresh flat-leaf parsley

⅓ cup chopped cilantro

⅓ cup chopped fresh dill

2 tablespoons chopped walnuts

1 tablespoon pine nuts

5 green cardamom pods, crushed, the black seeds retained and the pods discarded

sea salt and freshly ground black pepper

an 8-inch heavy nonstick skillet (measure the base, not the top)

serves 2–3

Heat 2 tablespoons of the oil in the skillet. Add the onion and cook for about 5 minutes, turning frequently, until beginning to soften. Add the eggplant and cook with the onion for another 5 minutes. Stir in the garlic and cook for 1 minute.

Meanwhile, break the eggs into a large bowl and beat lightly with a fork. Mix in the parsley, cilantro, dill, walnuts, pine nuts, black seeds from the cardamom pods, a little salt, and plenty of pepper. Remove the onion and eggplant from the skillet with a slotted spoon and add to the egg mixture. Stir well.

Add the remaining oil to the skillet and return to the heat. Add the tortilla mixture, spreading it evenly. Cook over medium-low heat until the bottom is golden brown and the top almost set.

Put a plate or flat saucepan lid on top of the skillet, then invert so the tortilla drops onto the plate or lid. Slide back into the skillet, brown side up, and cook for 2–3 minutes until lightly browned. Serve hot or at room temperature, cut into wedges.

Loaded with sausages, fried potatoes, and onions, this dish is perfect comfort food. Ring the changes with different kinds of sausage—try slices of chorizo, spicy Italian sausages, or even frankfurters.

sausage, potato, and onion tortilla

3–4 tablespoons extra virgin olive or safflower oil

6 pork chipolata sausages with herbs

1 onion

3 medium potatoes, about 12 oz., thinly sliced

5 extra-large eggs

sea salt and freshly ground black pepper

an 8-inch heavy nonstick skillet (measure the base, not the top)

serves 2–3

Heat 1 tablespoon of the oil in the skillet. Add the sausages and sauté for 8–10 minutes, turning them frequently. Remove and set aside. Wipe out the skillet with a paper towel.

Cut the onion in half and then into slivers lengthwise.

Heat 2 tablespoons of the oil in the cleaned skillet. Add the potatoes, layering them with the onions. Cook for 10–15 minutes over medium-low heat, lifting and turning occasionally, until just tender. The potatoes and onions should not brown very much.

Meanwhile, break the eggs into a large bowl, add salt and pepper, and beat lightly with a fork. Remove the potatoes and onions from the skillet with a slotted spoon and add to the egg mixture. Thickly slice the sausages and mix with the eggs and potatoes.

Return the skillet to the heat, adding a little more oil if necessary. Add the potato and egg mixture spreading it evenly. Cook over medium-low heat until the bottom is golden brown and the top has almost set.

Put a plate or flat saucepan lid on top of the skillet, then invert so the tortilla drops onto the plate or lid. Slide back into the skillet, brown side up, and cook for 2–3 minutes until lightly browned underneath. Serve hot or warm, cut into wedges.

There is nothing quite like the char-grilled flavor of roasted vegetables; as a tortilla filling they make a delicious alternative to the more traditional potato. You can roast the vegetables up to 24 hours in advance and keep chilled until you are ready to make the tortilla. Allow a little extra time to cook the tortilla, because the vegetables will be cold.

roasted vegetable tortilla

1 red onion, cut into wedges

1 red bell pepper, seeded and cut into thick strips

1 leek, thickly sliced

1 cup (4 oz.) butternut squash, cubed, or patty pans, sliced

6 sprigs of thyme

2 garlic cloves, unpeeled

3 tablespoons extra virgin olive or safflower oil

6 extra-large eggs

sea salt and freshly ground black pepper

a roasting pan

a 12-inch heavy nonstick skillet (measure the base, not the top)

serves 3–4

Put the onion, bell pepper, leek, and squash in large roasting pan. Sprinkle with thyme, salt, and pepper, bury the garlic cloves under the vegetables, and sprinkle with 2 tablespoons of the oil. Roast in a preheated oven at 400°F for 20 minutes, then turn the vegetables over and roast for a further 10 minutes.

Remove from the oven and let cool for 5 minutes. Remove the soft flesh from the roasted garlic and discard the skins. Discard the thyme stalks, removing any leaves still attached.

Break the eggs into a large bowl, add salt and pepper, and beat lightly with a fork. Add the vegetables and mix gently.

Heat the remaining oil in the skillet. Add the tortilla mixture and cook over medium-low heat for about 10 minutes or until the bottom is golden brown and the top almost set.

Put a plate or flat saucepan lid on top of the skillet, then invert so the tortilla drops onto the plate or lid. Slide back into the skillet, browned side up, and cook for 2–3 minutes until lightly browned underneath. Alternatively, slide under a preheated broiler to finish cooking the top. Let stand for 5 minutes to settle. Serve hot or at room temperature, cut into wedges.

index

conversion chart

Weights and measures have been rounded up
or down slightly to make measuring easier.

Volume equivalents:

American	Metric	Imperial
1 teaspoon	5 ml	
1 tablespoon	15 ml	
¼ cup	60 ml	2 fl.oz.
⅓ cup	75 ml	2½ fl.oz.
½ cup	125 ml	4 fl.oz.
⅔ cup	150 ml	5 fl.oz. (¼ pint)
¾ cup	175 ml	6 fl.oz.
1 cup	250 ml	8 fl.oz.

Weight equivalents: | **Measurements:**

Imperial	Metric	Inches	cm
1 oz.	25 g	¼ inch	5 mm
2 oz.	50 g	½ inch	1 cm
3 oz.	75 g	¾ inch	1.5 cm
4 oz.	125 g	1 inch	2.5 cm
5 oz.	150 g	2 inches	5 cm
6 oz.	175 g	3 inches	7 cm
7 oz.	200 g	4 inches	10 cm
8 oz. (½ lb.)	250 g	5 inches	12 cm
9 oz.	275 g	6 inches	15 cm
10 oz.	300 g	7 inches	18 cm
11 oz.	325 g	8 inches	20 cm
12 oz.	375 g	9 inches	23 cm
13 oz.	400 g	10 inches	25 cm
14 oz.	425 g	11 inches	28 cm
15 oz.	475 g	12 inches	30 cm
16 oz. (1 lb.)	500 g		
2 lb.	1 kg		

Oven temperatures:

110°C	(225°F)	Gas ¼
120°C	(250°F)	Gas ½
140°C	(275°F)	Gas 1
150°C	(300°F)	Gas 2
160°C	(325°F)	Gas 3
180°C	(350°F)	Gas 4
190°C	(375°F)	Gas 5
200°C	(400°F)	Gas 6
220°C	(425°F)	Gas 7
230°C	(450°F)	Gas 8
240°C	(475°F)	Gas 9